Thanks for the Memories

My Journey with Alzheimer's as a Caregiver to My Mother

M. JOANNE ROTH

authorHOUSE®

AuthorHouse™
1663 Liberty Drive
Bloomington, IN 47403
www.authorhouse.com
Phone: 1 (800) 839-8640

Scripture quotations marked NKJV are taken from the New King James Version.
Copyright © 1982 by Thomas Nelson, Inc. Used by permission. All rights reserved.

Published by AuthorHouse 02/15/2019

ISBN: 978-1-7283-0044-3 (sc)
ISBN: 978-1-7283-0043-6 (hc)
ISBN: 978-1-7283-0042-9 (e)

Library of Congress Control Number: 2019901812

Print information available on the last page.

Any people depicted in stock imagery provided by Getty Images are models,
and such images are being used for illustrative purposes only.
Certain stock imagery © Getty Images.

This book is printed on acid-free paper.

Because of the dynamic nature of the Internet, any web addresses or links contained in
this book may have changed since publication and may no longer be valid. The views
expressed in this work are solely those of the author and do not necessarily reflect the
views of the publisher, and the publisher hereby disclaims any responsibility for them.

Contents

Dedication

To my husband, Neil, who lovingly supported me through this journey, and to our daughter, Laurie, and son, Edward, who backed me with prayer and encouragement.

Foreword

There are many books outlining Alzheimer's with a scientific-biological explanation. The real treasure in this work by Joanne Roth is the reflection into the emotional-spiritual journey experienced by the Alzheimer's patient and the caretaker.

Memories are created as a result of life's experiences. We make decisions and plan our actions based on memories. Because the Alzheimer's patient has great difficulty with short-term memory, the individual's actions are no longer triggered by a recognition of his/her surroundings or relationships but rather by emotions––usually fear and frustration. Can you imagine trying to muddle your way through a new and unknown place or task, not just once a day, but all day––every day? Picture the impact on relationships. Can you journey spiritually through such troublesome days?

With this insightful look into the daily encounter with Alzheimer's, Joanne Roth's perspective and discernment probe these questions. This emotional-spiritual viewpoint is refreshing and very relevant in developing a fuller picture of the process we call Alzheimer's disease.

ANDREW CASTRODALE, M.D.
Family Practice
Grand Coulee, Washington

Introduction

To come home from shopping to find your home engulfed in flames would be a terrifying experience. The horror of that scene would intensify if you knew the fire department was unable to get a loved one out to safety. To go to the beach and watch a storm crash onto the rocks would be exhilarating until one of the waves unexpectedly swept over the top of you. Exhilaration would then turn to terror.

What if you discover you are losing your memory and your loss is accelerating to a point where basic needs are no longer able to be met? Everyday decisions gradually turn into living nightmares. "Why can't I figure out how to pay my bills? Why do I get lost so easily? Why is what used to be familiar so foreign now?" This ever-changing pattern creates the worst panic of all, not only for yourself but also for those looking on.

How many times are we faced with being out of control where some other force seems to take over and render us helpless? For the Christian, it might seem that God is not listening, is not aware of our needs, or just plain doesn't care. Where is God when adversity strikes? Can we trust His promises in all situations? Can He bring blessing out of chaos? Even senility?

Paul states in Philippians 4:19: "And my God shall supply all your need according to His riches in glory by Christ Jesus." How can this verse be reconciled with a disease such as Alzheimer's, where the brain is destroyed little by little until the individual becomes completely dependent on another person for his/her thoughts and survival? What is left to bring praise to the Lord when you have been reduced to only involuntary responses that might exhibit profanity or hostility? These are some of the difficult questions my heart wrestled with as I began to lose my mother, Hetty Weatherby, memory by memory.

This book is written to address these issues and to show God's love, grace, and mercy continually at work, regardless of life's deepest problems. It is also written to share my walk with God as a caregiver to my mother as she deteriorated with Alzheimer's disease. It is a praise to our wonderful, loving Lord in spite of this tragedy.

May you be inspired to let go of your seemingly impossible circumstances and let God show His power and love to you. He is always faithful and wants to bless those who love Him.

Chapter One

Early Warning Signs

It was early fall in 1987 when we received our first clue that something was wrong with Mom. We did not take it too seriously at the time, thinking it was just a one-time difficulty.

My husband, Neil, was pastoring a church in Langdon, North Dakota, and my time was divided between church work, mental health counseling, and teaching a number of piano students. Our two children were grown and on their own, so there were just the two of us. My father passed away in 1975, having suffered many years from asthma, pulmonary emphysema, and parkinsonism.

Mom remarried in 1979, but a few years later, her second husband, Xena, developed parkinsonism also. The two of them resided in Walla Walla, Washington, where she cared for him. It was during this time that we received a phone call from her that Xena had taken a bath and she did not know how to get him out of the bathtub. It seemed humorous to us at the time that she would call us in North Dakota, as though we could help her from that distance. She was at a total loss and somewhat panicked as to what to do. It never occurred to her to call my sister, June, who lived nearby or to ask help from a neighbor.

Early in 1988 Mom was unable to continue caring for Xena, so he was placed in a nursing home. She continued to go there three times a day for six months to feed him his meals and spend time with him. The stress was taking its toll, but we were not aware of how entangled it was with the beginning signs of Alzheimer's.

From time to time we received phone calls with questions on how to pay her bills. It was not so much a matter of finances as it was of how to write a check and process details. Her sense of organization was slipping. It was especially peculiar to me because she had taught me record-keeping skills. I could not understand her inability to do simple, ordinary things she had always been doing.

In July 1988, Xena passed away, and Mom was once again faced with being alone. The thought seemed to unduly frighten her, and we just assumed she was struggling with grief. We invited her to spend the winter with us in North Dakota to try to gain a new perspective. She was quick to accept our invitation.

Looking back, grief was only a part of the picture. While with us, she exhibited extreme paranoia about people stealing things from her. She would hide things to avoid theft and then forget where she put them. She had an unusual mistrust for professional people such as doctors, bankers, and lawyers, thinking they were somehow out to get her. Dental visits became a real chore because she would argue with the dentist's report and deny there was a problem.

After six months Mom wanted to return to Walla Walla. Hoping things would stabilize for her, we took her back. Within three months we realized her memory was continuing to deteriorate so that her concept of time, organization, and schedules no longer held any meaning. It was beginning to make sense why she was having so much trouble paying bills and preparing simple meals. Fortunately, she always maintained a good appetite.

There were no easy answers: June was not able to care for Mom, and there was no one else but us. Since she did not do well with the North Dakota winter weather, if we were to care for her, it would require our relocating to the Northwest.

After some investigation, it was apparent that no churches in our denomination were open in Oregon or Washington at the time, so we decided to inquire about like-faith denominations. The Lord opened a door for ministry in Auburn, Washington. After much prayer, we decided to make the pastoral change and have Mom move in with us.

Rather than arguing over breaking up her housekeeping and selling her home, she seemed quite relieved to come along with us. The Lord went before us each step of the way, preparing her mind and emotions for the change. It was hard to believe the whole process went so smoothly and without trauma for her.

Little did we know how precious the promise in Romans 8:28 would become to us: "And we know that all things work together for good to those who love God, to those who are called according to His purpose." The words **work together** have the meaning of "synchronizing things together," and if we ever needed that concept it was then. The "challenging" and the "mundane" were perfectly worked out into a beautiful mosaic. God's grace, given to us through His Son, Jesus Christ, became the seasoning that made the hard things palatable and gave meaning and purpose to everything.

One leading Christian man tried to convince us to place Mom in a nursing home rather than take her into our home so that the Lord could more fully use our talents in ministry. His thought was that her care would place great limitations on us. This idea may have seemed the most reasonable, but it was contrary to what we felt as the will of God for us. We chose to walk by faith and trust the Lord to "synchronize" the needs of the new church we were pastoring, Mom's needs, and our needs. We were confident that His promises were equally true for each one of us. We knew the circumstances could be overwhelming without the Lord's strength and wisdom but were willing to trust Him with all of the dynamics and details.

When first entering the ministry, we enrolled in the "School of Faith." Some lessons came easier than others. Many learned out of a textbook were quickly put to use. Others that were not fully understood needed to be taken by greater faith and required years of practice.

In addition, we needed a refresher course in the "School of Patience," for our home would become the classroom for intensified testing like never before. It is interesting what James says in Chapter 1, verses 2-4: "My brethren, count it all joy when you fall into various trials, knowing that the testing of your faith produces patience. But let patience have its perfect work, that you may be perfect and complete, lacking nothing." And yet, by nature, my tendency was to avoid circumstances that would lead to pain and discomfort. The Lord in His wisdom, however, allowed us to be confronted with this situation so He could produce much growth and blessing.

I am reminded of school days when I sometimes held until last the harder assignments, maybe thinking somehow they would just go away. Eventually deadline pressures forced me into the discipline of learning. Perhaps God was exercising a little pressure to develop Christian maturity in us so we could be more effective?

It is easy to feel we have had enough stretching in some areas, but we are ever learning as we walk the road of new circumstances. The question might be asked, "Are we really so wise that we should do the choosing of our circumstances?" I don't believe we would ever choose pain to develop Christian maturity.

Chapter Two

Attitude Adjustments

Caring for an Alzheimer's patient put my emotions on a roller coaster. The extreme memory loss impacted everything and everyone around us; change became the constant. I needed an attitude adjustment and a new vision through God's eyes to deal with this.

The first feeling I wrestled with was tied to denial. I knew Mom needed to be with us, but I wanted to believe that Alzheimer's only happened to other people. Surely what she had could be treated.

An appointment was made quickly with a specialist who conducted many tests. Every other possibility of disease was ruled out, and while a 100 percent diagnosis of Alzheimer's cannot be given until an autopsy is performed, she had all of the classic symptoms. It was necessary that we accept the doctor's report early on to be able to cope with the illness.

Feelings of anger flooded over me as I thought of how unfair this was for her––this was my mom. If she had just been some old reprobate, it might have been easier to accept. I thought of how she would be giving up everything, most of all her thinking capacity. She would be moving from independence to total dependence.

It was difficult to think of becoming the parent and Mom becoming the child. Besides, I still had so many things I wanted to learn from her and share with her. She always had so much to offer to others. No longer would I be able to share special moments and occasions with her. In a way, I felt I still needed her and wasn't ready to give her up, especially to something like this. She was being cheated out of life, and so was I. Were precious memories all that would be left?

Then I began to think selfishly of the freedom and things we would be giving up. How they paled in contrast to Mom's situation, however. It was great to have our children grown and on their own, but now we were going back into "childcare" in reverse and at a time when we were enjoying just being the two of us and looking forward to retirement within a short time. Some people call it the "Sandwich Generation."

Another concern was for our church in North Dakota; it was growing and revealed such potential. Why couldn't she adjust better to the very cold climate there? It would have been so much easier to bring her to North Dakota than to think of relocating just for her sake.

Still another issue was that my counseling degree had been completed only a few years earlier, and my counseling practice was going very well. Would all my training just be for nothing? And what about my many piano students? But could it be that some of my training was preparation for the events ahead?

Truly this was a time for soul searching. Praise the Lord, when we walk with Jesus, He does not leave us without answers and without hope. We are never put out on a limb for Him to chop it off behind us. He meets us where our needs are, where we hurt, where we lack understanding and good judgment. Proverbs 3:5-6 came to mind: "Trust in the Lord with all your heart, and lean not on your own understanding; in all your ways acknowledge Him, and He shall direct your paths." Well, we certainly needed direction.

I also thought of Psalm 37:4: "Delight yourself also in the Lord, and He shall give you the desires of your heart." How in the world could that be possible with these circumstances?

The impossible came true, however, as I asked Jesus to mold me into His image day by day. My attitude adjustment did not happen overnight, but continues as an ongoing process as I yield myself to Him daily, like clay in the hands of a potter. As a result, my desires were and continue to be transformed into His desires, and the preceding verses became a personal reality. We could both look to the future with joy even though uncertainties were present as to how the Lord would "synchronize" all the details. Fortunately we did not need to know "how" as much as to simply "trust and obey."

When I use the word **we** it is because my husband accepted the challenge as well and has been a very loving support throughout the experience. God may not assign everyone to this role, but we felt His call upon our lives and we accepted it, not out of duty but out of love.

Rather than looking at a negative future and having our lives put on hold, we were determined that we would view it simply as different than we had planned. "Different" does not mean good or bad. With this in mind, the Lord helped us make the necessary adjustments that allowed us to live our lives to the fullest and continue the ministry that was before us.

I often marvel at the creative mind of God. And wouldn't you know, He had wonderful things planned for us, things we could not have imagined let alone put together. He truly does care.

* * * * *

You may be wondering what attitude adjustments Mom needed to make. What was she feeling? Over the years the Lord gave her a warm, loving spirit which made it a joy to care for her. Memory loss, however, caused her to become easily and quickly dissatisfied and irrational. Her reality was always changing, and her tolerance level was diminishing greatly.

Worry became her constant companion. Originally we thought it might be a blessing for her to live in an imaginary world where worry and cares would be set aside, but she only exchanged real worries for imaginary ones.

She questioned me several different times about a "black hole" concept where it seemed like her life was being funneled. She was unable to describe the scene and always exhibited great fear and trepidation when discussing it. Rather than developing it further, I usually tried to bring comfort through a hug and then tried to change the subject.

Mom also had a sense several times that something was drastically wrong with her because she had trouble remembering her brother's and sister's names. She would ask what was wrong. While I did not try to shield her from the truth, a simple response always seemed sufficient, coupled with much reassurance that she was not alone. A cup of tea or hot chocolate would then be a welcome change.

Part of her daily routine was writing out her sibling's names and her birthday on any kind of paper that was available. Tablet paper was always in her room, but many times she bypassed it and tore pages out of books or albums. It did not seem to matter what she wrote on as much as the fact of going through the memory exercise. New sheets were found daily here and there in her room. It must have been a haunting fear that she would forget her family and birthday.

In addition, papers were found throughout her room of attempts to write letters to her mom and dad, who had died many years before. Since this held so much meaning for her, I would encourage her to write letters periodically, though nothing was completed. Just doing it meant a lot to her for the moment.

Her greatest attitude adjustment was not so much in giving up her home and coming to live with us or of mind deterioration but giving up her driving. I will address coping skills later in the book in that regard.

I never wanted Mom to feel abandoned. I cared, but I always knew God cared even more. My desired response was to keep trying to convey that great love.

Perhaps the most important ingredient in our relationship with Mom was a high level of trust. The Lord helped us maintain that throughout her sojourn with us. She seemed to feel at home and never once talked of going back to Walla Walla. It was as though that chapter had been erased from her memory. Her greatest needs were probably a sense of belonging and being loved, as well as safety and security. These we tried to provide with the Lord's help.

Chapter Three

The Pilgrimage Begins

We arrived at our new pastorate in Auburn, Washington, in November of 1989 with great excitement and joy. Much prayer preceded the unanimous call that was given to us.

The church put us up in temporary housing for a couple of months while we waited on the closing of a home we had purchased. Most of our things remained packed in boxes, and we made do with a few necessities. We called it the "Boxer Rebellion." The church was most helpful in supplying needs during our transition.

In December we went to Walla Walla to see how Mom was getting along, hoping that she would be all right until we could get settled in our new home in January. It did not take long, however, to realize that she needed help right then.

A look at her telephone bill revealed three pages of calls to check on the time. Monthly bills were not being paid. Her meals were about the same all the time and quite insufficient. She also expressed great apprehension about being alone.

We were none too early in caring for her. In spite of what seemed like poor timing, we were reminded that our loving Lord is always on time—never too early, and never too late.

We decided to take the rest of the week in getting her moved. This meant packing all her things, loading them in a U-Haul truck, cleaning her mobile home, putting it up for sale, and caring for any loose ends. It seemed an insurmountable task in such a short time, and all the while, I marveled at how she was processing these changes without any sense of questioning or hostility. I kept thinking that I would have been quite upset should one of our children have come in and started taking over my life. The Lord prepared her emotions in a marvelous way for what could have been so extremely traumatic, but she wasn't even asking any questions.

Our trip back to Auburn went very well. After arriving we decided to store Mom's things in the truck for the rest of the month and then move them directly to our new home, thus avoiding the handling of everything twice. The truck rental fee actually turned out to be cheaper than returning the truck and re-renting it again later. Isn't the Lord good!

Though we were in a temporary setting, Mom adjusted as though she had always been there with us. Nothing seemed unusual about the new arrangement to her. She did not question the change or ask about her things. It was as though her past life had been wiped out. Perhaps this w Lord's way of protecting her in her declining years anc whatever changes would take place in our lives.

December was an extremely busy month. January came quickly, and we were anxious to get settled in our new home. Much help was provided, making the transition a great deal easier. Again, Mom made the adjustment without question. What a praise to the Lord!

The next concern was what to do with all of her things as we were already crowded with our own belongings. We used the attached double garage as a staging area for "extras" which helped us avoid unnecessary confusion for Mom. She had no interest in going into the garage, so we were able to integrate what things we could over time and make other things available for a garage sale.

A friend was most helpful in taking Mom to her place during the sale. What did not sell was given to those in need. We were careful, however, to save whatever we thought would be meaningful to her and place it in her room and wherever else things would fit. Never once did she seem to miss anything that had been sold or given away.

Our home was located at the end of a cul-de-sac and was purchased with Mom in mind. There would be far less traffic with which to deal. A large bedroom with an adjacent bath was ideal for her needs. It was located at the front of the house.

Two large windows in her bedroom provided plenty of light and a lovely view of our front lawn and neatly landscaped flower beds, as well as other homes in the area. Mom enjoyed the seasonal changes of flowers but was especially delighted when spring produced its first rainbow of colors. Though the names of flowers were fading away, she was anxious for the crocuses, tulips, and daffodils to show off their splendor, followed by the glorious rhododendrons and azaleas.

A squirrel played vigorously in the front yard nearly every day, creating quite a drama for Mom. He would chatter away by the hour and then raise quite a ruckus when our Pomeranian would get too close. The nearby birch tree provided a quick retreat for the little fellow to scurry up and down.

Mom's room was easy to decorate. We chose a cheerful, apricot floral border print with a deep green background to edge the ceiling and built-in bookcases. The shelves were an ideal place to display her mementos, knickknacks, albums, scrapbooks, etc. Her bedspread and matching curtains had the same deep green background with more apricot floral designs.

Mom's walls were well suited for a collage of photos and memorabilia such as her LPN Certificate which she earned when she was in her early sixties. We were especially proud of her 4 point GPA and goal of working in nursing homes. Most of the pictures were of her family (Mom being the oldest of twelve children); my dad; June and her family; me and my family; and her second husband, Xena. Each person had always been very significant and special in her life.

It was not long after creating the wall displays that she began taking them down and mixing everything up. Little did I know she was unable to attend to very many things at once and that already my childhood was gone from her memory bank. It was important that I focus on that which she was capable of rather than what I thought she would enjoy based on my enjoyment or appreciation.

The size of her room allowed for a double bed, double dresser, night stand, rocker, desk, and two trunks. She also had a television set and stereo system. Music almost always flowed from her room, where she spent much of her time. She had a great appreciation for music but was never given the opportunity to develop her innate talent. Since June and I were given music lessons, perhaps Mom received her musical education vicariously.

Early on we discovered her tendency to wander off, not knowing how to return home. We decided to put an alarm system in our home that would let us know if a window or door was violated so we did not have to be continually "on guard."

An ID bracelet was also ordered for her with her name, our address and phone number, and the designation of Alzheimer's written on it. I was unsure of how she would respond to wearing it, but she seemed delighted. It was quite easy to place it on her, and I was mindful that it needed to be there permanently so she could not get it off. She must have thought of it as just jewelry. How thankful I was. We never wanted her to feel embarrassment about her disease.

After Mom was somewhat settled in her new surroundings, we went to the bank and made sure all of her funds were in joint accounts with her, June, and me. How much easier this has been for paying her bills. Should something have happened so I could not continue as the primary caregiver, June would have been able to take over Mom's finances. That never became necessary, but at least the option was available and prearranged.

Another very important asset was acquiring durable power of attorney for June and me. Fortunately, this had been done while she was still of sound mind and allowed us freedom to make necessary decisions on Mom's behalf. It was especially important with regard to medical attention needed. Without the power of attorney, even though I was the caregiver, I would not have been entitled to information from doctors even on simple concerns. A trustee would have been appointed to make decisions and address her needs, and I may or may not have been the one selected; even a spouse is not automatically assigned the role of trustee.

One final issue was that of her car title. Mom had been a Washington State resident for the past two years but still maintained an unexpired California driver's license while using Washington license plates. Her car insurance agent did not pick up on this, and she was none the wiser.

When her car insurance came up for renewal, we went in to pay her bill and found that it could not be renewed without the driver's license change, and we knew she would be required to take a written test that she would never be able to pass. In order to continue to insure her car, it became necessary that she transfer the title to our names which she seemed most happy to do. This again could have been a most difficult situation, but the Lord went before us and managed every detail.

Since a joint bank account, power of attorney, and car title transfer require the individual making the changes to be of sound mind, it is extremely important that these changes take place early on with regard to any mind-deteriorating diseases. Actually, in our case, the joint bank accounts and power of attorney were acquired several months before the Alzheimer's was even suspected. With regard to the car title change, her willing cooperation was so apparent that no questions were asked. Again, the Lord was in charge before we even knew the need would exist.

Chapter Four

Historical Snapshots

ᏧᎳᎤᎤ

To better understand some of the dynamics of Mom's deterioration, it is helpful to know some of her background. She was born and raised on a small farm near Mitchell, Oregon, in 1912. Having been two months premature at birth. her weight was guessed at about two pounds. It was said that her head would fit into a small teacup.

By 1933 eleven other siblings had come along, making a total of six boys and six girls. Her father struggled to make a living farming, but while they were poor financially, the family was rich in a closeness for each other which continues to this day through annual reunions and a "round robin" letter which circulates about every three months.

Being the oldest child in the Vaughan family, Mom was thrust into an adult role of responsibility early in life as she helped care for her brothers and sisters. Her mother was warm and loving but somewhat crippled and needy.

The children walked or rode horses several miles to a one-room schoolhouse. Sometimes the Vaughan kids were the only students present. Grades one through eight met together with one teacher; high school was not available there.

Mom married Albert Rue (my father) on April 10, 1930. He had been a school teacher at the same school she attended earlier. After school was out that summer, they moved to Monument, Oregon, where he helped his dad run his farm. He also worked at lumber mills, then attended Monmouth Normal School and many years later Eastern Oregon College of Education. He spent the rest of his career teaching the fourth grade in The Dalles, Oregon, and finally retired in 1966 with poor health.

Three children were born to my folks: John Leroy, who was killed by a train at age ten; me, and June Lucille.

Finances were tight, so Mom felt the need to work outside the home. She spent a number of years working at the local T.B. hospital as a nurse's aide. When it closed she continued working in a dry cleaning business.

In 1971 my folks were persuaded to move to Walla Walla, Washington, where we were living at the time. We wanted to be able to help with my dad's failing health.

Mom took her GED from Walla Walla Community College and enrolled in a nursing program. After receiving her LPN degree with honors at age sixty-two, she worked many years in rest homes. My dad passed away in 1975.

Mom married Xena Weatherby in 1979 and moved to Fresno, California. In 1986 they moved back to Walla Walla, where June resided. Xena's health was slipping, and they wanted to be close to family. In 1988 he passed away. Little did we know Alzheimer's was already making inroads on Mom's health.

With this quick historical sketch, you may be wondering what kind of person Mom was prior to Alzheimer's and what changes took place. She was a very caring, loving, no-nonsense person but maintained a good sense of humor. She cared for some of her siblings even after she was married. She was a primary caregiver to both husbands. She cared enough about people in general to begin her LPN degree when she was sixty-one and spent many years working in rest homes instead of retiring.

She was a Christian wife and mother, spilling love on all those around her. She encouraged godly values. Though never perfect, she always did the best she could in every situation.

She learned to make do with little. I especially think back to two incredible stories. When my folks had been married only a few years, they decided to move from Mitchell, Oregon, to Prineville, Oregon, with a very beat-up old car. Times were so tough that when the tires wore out, they continued the trip into Prineville on the rims.

A second story finds them relocating in The Dalles, Oregon, some years later and in need of housing. Still times were tough, not just financially, but also because of World War II and limited building materials. The folks had enough money, however, to purchase some property and then were awarded a contract to tear down an old hotel in the town which would provide much of the lumber for the building of their home. In addition, the nails were carefully removed, straightened, and reused.

Mom learned to cope with the death of a ten-year-old son, the death of a younger brother in World War II, and the loss of two husbands. As a daughter, I am quick to "rise up and call her blessed" (Proverbs 31:28).

In spite of her early childhood adult role, Mom seemed to be quite well rounded. She was a joy to be with and to take on family vacations. She had a great sense of humor and enjoyed church, sewing, and sacred and classical music. June and I were given music lessons and attended many concerts. Mom seemed to have a natural talent for music herself but was never given the opportunity to develop it.

As to her physical characteristics: she was 5'5" tall; maintained about one hundred twenty pounds; had dark brown hair, clear blue eyes, and wore glasses; and had nice features and a good complexion. Though she did not always exude a high degree of self-confidence, her inner beauty and integrity always complemented her outer beauty.

Chapter Five

The Downhill Journey

Because Alzheimer's is such a debilitating, unpredictable disease, it was necessary as a caregiver that I look beyond myself. I had to pray for increased faith, guidance, wisdom, and patience. My ability was exhausted so quickly, but the Lord always came through with faithful answers and always on time. So often the response was there before I even knew the problem was ready to surface.

Most of this discussion will be related to the multiplied effects of Mom's memory loss and some of the coping skills we found helpful.

Loss of Organization

It was evident when we first realized Mom was unable to care for herself any longer that she, too, was aware of some of the memory loss that was taking place. She became very frightened and agitated with her inability to care for routine things such as paying bills and preparing meals. Her sense of organization was being replaced by confusion.

Normal responsibilities made little sense. A budget, menu, recipe, or list of items lost their meaning. Dressing became more difficult as she tried to determine what went where and when. Equally difficult for her was knowing what to do with her clothes when they were taken off, let alone how to take them off. She would try to hang up hosiery and socks. A dress or blouse might be found wadded up with books on a shelf. Her closet and dresser drawers, which I cleaned and organized often, were quickly thrown into chaos with no rhyme nor reason. She truly reminded me of a pack rat trying to put a nest together, only her efforts were no longer with any purpose or meaning.

Confusion with Eating

Mom never lacked for an appetite, nor was she a fussy eater, for which I was most thankful. It was great to see her enjoy her meals because she had so little she really could enjoy. I always tried to make them as appealing as possible. We also shared snacks with her at different times.

It was not long, however, before Mom's confusion spread to her eating. Many times, having just finished a meal, she would ask when we were going to eat. It was no big deal to her when we would remind her we had already eaten. Usually

I would hand her an apple or cookie as follow-up anyway. Fortunately, weight was never a problem for her.

You may be wondering about the safety of a kitchen stove and other appliances. The knobs on our stove were located at the back and required pushing in before turning. She never could figure out how to use them, though one had been broken from her efforts. Other kitchen appliances did not make any sense to her, so we could relax somewhat with the kitchen.

Loss of Sense of Time

In a quick review of Mom's telephone bill, three pages were devoted to calls for the correct time, with many of them being placed only minutes apart. It was not a matter of the correct time not being available, for there were many clocks throughout the house and she always wore a wristwatch. A sense of time had become elusive for her.

The concept of what day, week, month, or year it was also was scrambled in her mind. Appointments had little meaning; morning and evening activities became mixed up. What were a few minutes to us became a few hours to her. As a result, impatience began to interfere more and more so that her attention span became less and less. This was not all bad, however, because a belligerent spirit which surfaced from time to time could be fairly easily replaced with a more compliant spirit merely by changing the subject or focus.

Dread of Being Alone

It was one thing for Mom to have lost a second husband in death, but to begin to see so many other losses taking place in her own life, it was no wonder she was reluctant to stay alone. She no longer felt secure with decision making, common sense, and good judgment. Very simple responsibilities such as fixing a meal or paying routine bills were overwhelming her.

Paranoia

I remember, from my childhood, a lack of trust that Mom had for many authority figures such as doctors, lawyers, bankers, and businessmen in general. She always felt they were out to get her. She was convinced they were more concerned about making money than they were with her needs. They would create problems in order to have something to fix. These feelings were greatly amplified with Alzheimer's, making it difficult to meet some of her professional needs such as dental work.

It became necessary that we avoid sharing very much information with her concerning appointments so she would not catastrophize upcoming events. It was easier to schedule an outing with errands attached to it. This was much more acceptable to her and did not allow time to set up negative, argumentative thinking.

Another paranoia Mom exhibited was that someone was always trying to steal things from her. She hid things continually but never in likely places. Because her sense of organization had been so diminished, we could not be sure if the "jumble" of things in her room was common sense gone awry or the attempt at hiding things.

Periodically paranoia was evidenced by the threatening people she saw reflected in windows and mirrors, especially in the evening. Whether these apparitions were paranoia, hallucinations, or mere lack of recognition of the reflection of herself or others in the room, they were very frightening and real to her.

Reasoning went nowhere with her. There were times when it was necessary to shut the blinds and cover her dresser mirror to calm her down. Eventually we removed all mirrors from her room. The mirror in her bathroom was much smaller and never seemed to bother her so we left it in place.

Argumentation

Because I wanted to minimize stress for all of us, and since we knew Mom was unable to problem solve anymore, we knew that discussion or counseling was of little value. The only problem with that was my tendency to want to try to correct Mom's irrational thinking.

The desire to be right and correct her troubled world soon lost its pull, however. As long as Mom's imaginary world did not affect her safety, being right or wrong no longer needed to be an issue. We went along with her in her "dream world" where we could and changed the subject or surrounding where necessary. It was fairly easy to distract her with a snack or something to drink such as hot chocolate.

Many were the times I role-played with Mom to prevent argument. It was the lesser of two evils to pick berries off the floor that were not there; to carry on an imaginary conversation; to graciously accept the home, which we had purchased, as though it had always belonged to her and she wanted to give it to us; to realize that my identity was long gone and many times I became her brother, Earl. This I took as a compliment, however, because I knew how much he meant to her.

It is not always safe to live in an illusionary world, nor do we always have the luxury of time to restructure a difficult situation. Such was the case one winter afternoon in January.

About a foot of snow blanketed the area providing a beautiful black-and-white landscape. The temperature had plummeted to about 10 degrees Fahrenheit, just above zero. Only those with serious needs would go out in this cold weather.

We lived in a residential neighborhood, but Mom was certain we were living on the farm on which she grew up. All of a sudden, in her shirt-sleeves, she was heading out the front door to feed horses that were not there. Physical restraint became necessary when she turned combative; reasoning went nowhere. Our hope was that with a different focus once again her mindset would change because of her low attention span. The issue at hand was always forgotten almost as quickly as it came up.

Boredom

So many of the characteristics of Alzheimer's are intertwined. I found that a short attention span mixed with boredom created or bred dissatisfaction. The inability to focus and complete a given task led to boredom and a desire to do something else. It also tended to produce a complaining and negative spirit. As we were trying to cope with some of these problems, we realized that Mom was also trying to cope, but in very irrational ways. Her mental abilities no longer matched her desires.

It was a real challenge as to how to keep Mom's life meaningful and satisfying. She never cared for television, and her mind didn't seem to track what was going on in a program anyway. Her confusion affected her ability to read as well. Familiar music seemed to be a welcome friend but was more of a background enjoyment. She needed things to do and quite often wanted to be of help.

Dusting gave her a great satisfaction as she moved the cloth over the furniture. She would dust whatever came to mind, whether it was appropriate or not, but it did occupy her time and made her feel important. She always seemed to enjoy folding clothes from the laundry, but there was never any organization to what she did, so later on I would refold them and put them away. She did not know she was not a big help.

She also looked forward to vacuuming the carpet but had trouble remembering where she had been and where she needed to go. Her work was very inadequate, but again we tried to boost her ego with how much help she had been. Sooner or later she would be tearing the vacuum apart even though nothing was wrong. Eventually it was destroyed before I had a chance to intervene.

Mom had a history of repairing many things in the past out of necessity. The only problem now was that she wanted to fix things that were not broken.

She had a very prized hurricane lamp on her night stand. One day I found her tearing it to pieces. The light bulb had burned out, but she was reliving her childhood when oil lamps were used. Surely it was out of oil and needed refilling. If she could just find out where to put the oil that she didn't have. We were glad matches were not available to her. Who knows where her efforts might have gone.

A very lovely Fisher stereo set was at her disposal in her room so she could enjoy her old records whenever she wanted to. It played very well, but it was a puzzle to me that she extracted and ruined expensive needles periodically. We must have gone through six needles in three months. We wanted her to have as much autonomy as possible but discovered too late that she had finally yanked the arm off the stereo. It was completely trashed, again the desire to fix something that was already working well.

Mom had a great appreciation for simple jewelry. One Mother's Day we bought her a lovely necklace. Later in the afternoon I found her at the dining room table cutting it into little pieces. It was never clear to me what she was trying to fix at that time, but it did initiate the end of jewelry for her. She no longer recognized its purpose and how to care for it. Fortunately, anything out of sight seemed to be out of mind as well, so there was never any question about it.

Another day I found her cutting individuals out of family pictures that she no longer recognized. Picture albums had always been highly treasured by Mom, but they became a muddle in her mind. We put them away in order to save them. Little by little her world (her room) was being reduced to what she could handle. It was especially apparent that scissors must not be readily available anymore either.

Perhaps my most helpful resource against boredom for her came in the form of crossword puzzles. These held her interest for long periods of time and were especially helpful when I went shopping or had appointments.

For a couple of years shopping was a joint project. She didn't mind the short trips, but I could tell she was disoriented in a store when confronted with the many aisles and multitudes of shelved goods. She spoke of a fear of things caving in on her, but her spirit would calm down when she pushed a shopping cart. Even though onlookers might have criticized me for having her push the cart, I could tell it was a great comfort to her. Again, it gave her something to do, a feeling of importance, and a sense of stability.

Eventually the disorientation increased and she felt more comfortable staying in the car for short periods of time while I did errands. It was then that the crossword puzzles captured her attention and held her interest until I returned. How thankful I was for this resource.

Crossword puzzles became too difficult after a few months, so we went down a step to word seek puzzles. This, too, captivated her until letters and words ceased to hold any more recognition for her. At this point, I didn't feel safe leaving her unattended for even a moment.

Wandering

In spite of the alarm system in our home, Mom managed to wander off three times. An identification bracelet became crucial, and we also made our neighborhood aware of her disease and potential wandering. This provided extra eyes and ears as well as search parties when needed. I can't speak highly enough of all of our neighbors and the people in our church who assisted us many times.

It was after Mom's last wandering that two different ladies in our church volunteered to take care of Mom once a week. One lady took her to her home for the day, and the other lady picked her up in the evening for an overnight visit. What a blessing! The Lord knew how much we needed help.

The first night we were alone, we realized how little sleep we had been getting. Our ears were trained to catch each little sound in case there was trouble. Unfortunately Mom never did require much more than about five or six hours of sleep, so morning always came very early.

I began to make the most of my free day each week, catching up with shopping and any other appointments that needed to be met.

Close friends also came to our home to stay with Mom for a few hours from time to time, but it was very difficult for the one in charge to maintain control because Mom thought she should be in charge on her own turf. She was much more compliant when cared for in someone else's place. This was a very important concept for us and those who wanted to be of help.

I remember how frustrated Mom would become when friends seemed to know where the dishes were in the cupboards better than she did. Even though she could no longer find even the obvious in the kitchen, such as where the sink was, she maintained a sense that she should know where everything was and she wanted to be in control.

Complaining/Negative Spirit

A large part of Mom's complaining spirit was probably due to her lack of self-confidence. Decisions were never easy for her. She was seldom satisfied with her choices. Almost every mail order item she would purchase was returned to the manufacturer. Seldom was she pleased with what she ordered. It was as though she didn't trust her own judgment or intuition. If someone else ordered the same thing, it would have been more than acceptable.

In addition, she seemed to feel unworthy of having nice things. She never wanted to stand out, to wear anything that would generate a compliment. She had trouble accepting praise. On the other hand, she did not want to stimulate criticism. She preferred to be like the majority and blend in. These feelings seemed to be amplified with Alzheimer's.

Mom was especially self-conscious with how she looked. As she got older, her arms seemed too thin, and she refused to wear anything less than a three-quarter length sleeve even on the hottest day. Wrinkles bothered her more than being comfortable. I tried to respond to her preferences even to making many of her clothes because long-sleeved garments were hard to come by in the summer.

As Alzheimer's advanced, the focus of criticism seemed to transfer from herself to us. This was difficult because Mom had always been so supportive of our decisions and choices in the past. It became increasingly difficult to please her. Perhaps it was another area in which she felt she was losing control.

Many was the time we had to overlook our differences with Mom and go ahead with that which was expedient. We continued to live in a particular time frame whether she did or not. Once a decision was set in motion, however, she tended to let go of the conflict. She always seemed able to adjust and was usually pleased with the end result.

Such was the case when we took her out to dinner once a week. There were times when she would react almost violently to going out, but when we arrived at our destination she would settle right down and seem to enjoy the evening. Fortunately there were few scenes in public, with the exception of eating, such as cutting her roll with a knife and fork and eating her potatoes and meat with her fingers.

Another area of conflict was between Mom and my private counseling practice, which was conducted in our home. The first year ran smoothly enough. She managed to entertain herself in her bedroom while I went through my sessions, but as time went by, her attention span became shorter and she seemed to be jealous of my time spent with other people. Argumentative interruptions forced me to put my practice on hold.

Fortunately, her compliance with the church was never in question. How beautifully the Lord prepared her for each service and each Bible study. We were especially blessed that she appeared quite normal in public. As long as conversation with her did not require answers other than "yes" or "no," few people would really suspect anything being wrong. Comments which required thought brought pressure to bear and she would start to fragment, yet she did not seem to be afraid to mingle with people.

She was most cooperative in helping us arrange for the church service. Chairs needed to be set up and hymn books distributed. She seemed to look forward to helping in any way she could.

We were always able to be on time for the needs of the church. One Sunday, however, after dressing Mom and getting everything ready to go, when I returned for her, she was back in her nightgown. Even that day we were able to accomplish what was needed in a timely manner and without argument.

Coping with the many changes required much flexibility in my expectations and many attitude adjustments. Mom's memory loss affected nearly everything and was always in a state of flux. It became increasingly difficult to anticipate behavior. About the time one area was getting under control, another loss would take place. A common question that surfaced was, "When did this loss happen?"

Loss of Appropriateness

With regard to routine and appropriateness, it was essential that we keep our expectations extremely flexible as different changes and losses took place regularly. Change became the norm, yet we needed to maintain a degree of orderliness to continue our roles. Flexibility was the key to peace as opposed to angering over what maybe "should have been." Many times our priorities needed restructuring. Perhaps this question helped as much as anything: "What is really important when all is said and done?"

Inappropriateness was most evident in Mom's confusion with clothes: what to wear on the inside and what to wear on the outside, when to wear appropriate clothes, such as nightwear versus daywear. Underclothes were often put on last. Her final bout with pantyhose was when she cut them off at the ankles rather than taking them off. She no longer understood the process of dressing and undressing.

Mom disappeared into her bedroom from one of our Bible studies only to reappear in her nightgown, wrong side out, a few minutes later. Fortunately, at least she was dressed, usually gracious, and well received whether she was proper or not. Again we were so thankful for the guests' patience and understanding. We felt great support, as opposed to criticism.

Daily I tried to bring organization to her room, but it immediately became chaos. Downsizing was necessary from time to time to keep up with her new limitations.

Another inappropriate behavior has already been briefly alluded to with regard to her confusion with eating, but we tried not to make her a spectacle in public. We never treated her difficulties with embarrassment because we knew she was doing the best she could. We would assist where needed and trust that other people would understand more than they would be offended. Her pleasantness usually captured the heart.

Still another behavioral problem took me quite by surprise. A very lovely and intricately crocheted doily was yanked off the dresser and Mom began to blow her nose on it. Another time a quilt was being torn to pieces for the same purpose. Kleenex tissue was always available for her but apparently no longer held any meaning.

Disorientation

Wandering was mentioned earlier in this chapter, but further clarification on disorientation may be helpful. It is not unusual to become lost in a shopping mall or parking lot;

it is a problem, however, if you cannot recognize the block in which you live, let alone the specific home.

Once Mom was out our front door, she was bewildered. One day our next door neighbor brought her wastebasket over to us, kindly directed Mom inside, and said she had lost her way. Apparently she had slipped out the front door and was picking up fall leaves in her wastebasket but could not find the door again. After wandering into the home next door, she was busily going through cupboards as though it was where she belonged. The young gentleman seemed to understand and was most protective of her when directing her back home.

Mom also became disoriented within our home. She could be in the kitchen but not know where the refrigerator was. Since she was reliving her childhood more and more, she may have thought back to her time without electric refrigerators, indoor sinks, and running water. She also had trouble finding the bathroom, but as a child, her family used outdoor plumbing. Finding her bedroom and discovering where her bed was became a challenge.

The confusion that surrounded Mom's disorientation was increasing. Her recognition of that which was most familiar to her was becoming a jumble. Shopping made less and less sense. Her loss of organization caused everything to run together and overwhelm her. Stores were no longer "people friendly" but began to exhibit qualities of a nightmare. Shopping routines were quickly fading away.

A dread of travel began to permeate our trips. It was apparent that not only did shelves of merchandise create instability for her but the passing of scenery also created disorder. This made her quite agitated and fearful. It was as though life had lost its steadiness and she was out of control. She struggled to attend to more than one thing at a time; this was becoming especially true of conversation as well. Overload needed to be kept to a minimum.

It soon became apparent that outings and vacations which previously had been such a joy for her were no longer the blessing we thought they would be. We tried to take her on a scenic trip in our mini-home. We could remember the many wonderful excursions we had taken in the past with her and were so excited about getting her out into nature once again. How shocked we were at the disaster the trip turned out to be. After only about forty miles, we returned home defeated, realizing she could not cope with travel anymore. The chronic grumbling played on like a broken record the whole return trip. This was not like her but was the reality she was moving into more and more. We were still discovering the triggers that would set her off, and, of course, they were ever changing.

We found ourselves learning selective hearing as we tuned out some of the unpleasantries. This made us more able to tolerate the complaining on short trips because we knew the end results were still so rewarding, such as taking Mom out to dinner once a week, going to a park, participating in church activities, going on small errands, visiting a friend, or taking in a concert.

Most of the time Mom was affable and composed in public. How grateful we were that negative scenes were not rehearsed in public very often.

Agitation and Hostility

Mom was never an aggressive type of person until Alzheimer's took its toll. Without any provocation, she would lash out in fistfights and scratch like a cat; usually it was when my back was turned. Neil would ask where all the bruises came from. I never was able to ascertain the cause of her hostility as it was never due to an argument. It just seemed to come out of nowhere. Fortunately, she never went through a stage of profanity.

There were times when I regretted the harsh words which left my lips, and how I wished they could have been taken back. My only comfort was that she would not remember, but I could remember and sought her forgiveness as well as the Lord's. I knew the way I treated her was also the way I was treating the Lord.

My best defense was just to watch my backside and try to change her emotion when she erupted. This difficult stage was short-lived, so again we had something for which to be thankful.

Catastrophize Pain

Fortunately, Mom was always physically very healthy. She never had been in the hospital, not even to deliver her three children. She did not even have a cold or flu in the four years she lived with us and experienced no arthritis or headaches. She wore glasses but maintained her own teeth.

She did, however, have bunions and corns which required a lot of attention. Keeping her feet in good shape required daily care. One time, I gave a little too much attention to one of her corns. It became infected and required antibiotics to clear it up. In addition to keeping the corns trimmed and soft, I tried slip-on cushioned toe dividers that seemed to help a lot.

In the past, Mom always had a very high tolerance for pain, but Alzheimer's changed that. She became like a child, catastrophizing every little discomfort as though she must immediately get to the hospital. Many were the evenings she would stand at our bedroom door yelling of pain. She could not tell you where it hurt, which made it difficult to know if something was wrong or not. My test was that if I could change the subject without the pain continuing, then I assumed it was imaginary or insignificant. Sometimes I gave her Tylenol, hoping it would help settle her down. Also, a cup of tea was a good pacifier.

Catastrophize Noise

Mom's ears seemed to become more sensitive to sound. Noises such as shutting the door too hard or dropping something in the sink would unnerve her. The sounds did not need to be catastrophic to cause her alarm and set her into mega questioning. She began to lose her cool in the face of normal everyday living.

Obsessions

Bowels

Because Mom had a lazy bowel most of her life, her system was nearly maxed out from the harsh laxatives and enemas which she had taken for years. The habit was very difficult to deal with because she expected to continue in the same lifestyle.

I knew her need was legitimate, but my desire was to shift to Metamucil type products, plenty of grains and cereals, prune juice, and plenty of liquids. In addition, we took two-mile walks every morning, which she always seemed to enjoy.

Even though we were trying a new program for her bowels, her mind refused to let go of the laxatives she had been taking for years. It was also complicated by the fact that she would forget when she had taken a pill and immediately insist on more. Furthermore she would forget when she had a bowel movement, and this would trigger her desire for a pill. She was never what you would consider a hypochondriac, but we were dealing with a real obsession. Placebos in the form of vitamin C were used often and did help placate the problem.

Because of Mom's need for some kind of help with her bowels and the drastic change we were trying to implement, it was important that I monitored her regularity. This was not easy because she could not remember to alert me to the situation. In fact, later on she became so obsessed with her feces that I would find bits and pieces on shelves, in drawers, mixed in with clothes, etc. It was as if she was saving them for some treasured purpose. She had developed a fixation on her bowels that only went from bad to worse.

Mom began to spend inordinate amounts of time in the bathroom. One afternoon I was thrown into a panic as I went to see what the ruckus was. She had jiggled so hard on the toilet seat that she had created a prolapsed rectum. Having never seen anything like it, I thought her insides were coming out so rushed her to the hospital. They didn't seem to be too alarmed over it, pushed the rectum back in place and showed me how to deal with it should it ever happen again.

Though we felt we had provided pretty good regularity for Mom, the bowel obsession remained our greatest challenge throughout her stay with us.

Carrying a purse

Many of these obsessions seemed to have been born out of years of habit, and they never lost their momentum. Because carrying a purse was more of a nuisance for us at this point than a necessity, I tried to leave it behind, but it was never out of her mind. Therefore we decided to use her purse as a crutch for her but removed everything of value. That way she felt more complete, and if the purse was misplaced, it presented no real problem; we would just get her another one. It was interesting that Mom never questioned what was or was not in her purse; it was just that she felt partially dressed without it.

Wearing a wristwatch

Mom's wristwatch was another constant companion. She was forever checking the time and trying to fix it even though it operated just fine. Having it with her all the time was what was important, not whether it continued to function properly.

Caring for her cat

This became very difficult because whatever she did for herself, she would do for the cat. One time I remember her trying to give laxatives to the cat on the basis of her own needs. Thankfully it was discovered before completion. For the safety of the cat, it eventually became necessary that we find another home for it. Because she had had the cat only a few years, the change did not create a problem.

Mega desire to drive

This was the most traumatic loss of all for Mom. Nothing else measured up to this. She always loved to drive and had never had an accident.

How fortunate we were that we discovered she was driving illegally. When moving to Walla Walla, Washington, from Fresno, California, she brought with her a five-year driver's license not knowing that after thirty days of residency in Washington she would need to have a Washington driver's license. She had already been in Walla Walla for two years and was still using her California license.

Knowing that she has always been quick to comply with the law, every time she wanted to drive I would remind her that she would be illegal until she had acquired a Washington driver's license. I would make myself available to help her study up for the test, something I knew she could not pass. Somehow I think she knew down deep she could not pass it either. Anyway, we went through this process about three times and then the desire seemed to fade away. How wonderful to be able to skirt the issue rather than telling her "no."

We used her car often because she was familiar with it and we thought she would feel more at home with it. It was interesting one day, however, when out of the blue she asked why we had gotten rid of her car. Actually, I guess she was thinking back to an earlier car she had owned before she married Xena. We had quite a time convincing her that this was the same car she came to us with. Somehow the subject changed and it never came up again.

Aversion to Hygiene

Gradually Mom became quite uncooperative with routine hygiene. Perhaps this was due to her loss in understanding the process of bathing and brushing teeth. Whatever the reason, it seemed to smooth out when I assisted her with baths, etc., rather than leaving her alone to do it on her own.

As time went on, I could never trim Mom's nails to suit her even though she had always worn them rather short in the past. It was a matter of just keepin' on and overlooking the hostility. Discussion did very little good.

Hair appointments were made for both of us at the same time. This worked very well since my presence seemed to provide a calming effect. Actually, washing her hair and styling it did not present much of a problem anyway. That was a special blessing.

Since dressing required assistance, dirty clothes were always removed immediately from her room when they were taken off. This kept argument to a minimum when it came time to dress again. Otherwise, the same clothes would have been worn over and over again.

Aversion to New Things

It did not take long to realize that familiar things were more appreciated and comfortable to Mom than new things. Old clothes were always preferred to new ones. Recognition was more important to her than whether an item was worn out and needed discarding. This was true of about anything.

It took her awhile to get used to a new bedspread, but her old one was for a king size bed. If it had not been quite old, I would have cut it down to fit a double bed size.

Music was another area of appreciating the old. She liked things she could recognize and go away singing or humming. She became quite agitated with much of the modern pop music with its booming sounds and undiscernible lyrics. Sacred and classical music were the most enjoyable to her.

Pacing

Pacing occurred many times during the day and night. Mom reminded me of a father waiting for a baby to be born. She would walk from one end of the room to the other and then do it over again and again. Her expression was not so much of anxiety as it was of a blank slate. It was a bit disconcerting at night since she could have fallen so easily.

Again the Lord protected her from any accidents, and she usually went back to bed on her own. We were also thankful for the security system in our home.

Loss of Communication

The first time Mom used nonsense syllables in her speech, she looked at me with some degree of confusion and asked if I understood what she had said. With a twinkle in my eye, I replied, "Well, not exactly." She started laughing and said, "I didn't either. Let me try again." It was interesting that she was aware of her fragmentation at that point. Garbled speech did not happen often at that time, but within a year began to deteriorate more and more. She had a great sense of humor, so it was used often to help diffuse some of the problems.

Grinding Teeth

Toward the last part of our four-year sojourn with Mom, she developed a habit of grinding her teeth, much like some people who bite their fingernails. We were glad she still had her own teeth since dentures would probably have often been misplaced. Deterioration of her teeth was a concern, however, so we began giving her chewing gum, hoping she would not swallow it and it would relieve some of her anxiety. It seemed to work well and when we gave her a snack, the gum was dropped automatically.

Chapter Six

Overview Of Coping Skills

Some of the difficulties we experienced might be very different from another person, so I can only share with you what worked for us. That which can be claimed as common ground, however, is the need to place total trust in the Lord for direction in meeting the ever-changing needs that surface.

As I thought of the high potential for anxiety and stress, I couldn't help but think of new meaning for the word *fear*:

Fighting battles alone
Entertaining negative aspects
Aborting faith and hope
Retreating from the battle.

Fortunately my husband was very supportive and helpful when needed, so this battle was never fought alone but together with the Lord. Though I did not belong to a specific Alzheimer's support group, our neighbors and church group assisted us in many ways. Rather than living an isolated existence, we continued to be involved with others through Bible studies, church activities, and various outings. There were also adult daycare centers sponsored by some churches that were available for several hours two or three days a week. I did not use this service but would highly recommend it.

To avoid "burnout," it was essential that we separate ourselves from the situation from time to time. We were not superhuman and could have become part of an additional problem by not listening to our own needs in the process of caregiving. Knowing our emotional and physical limitations helped us discern when "escape" was needed to gain new strength and perspective.

It is easy to entertain negative aspects with this disease because there is no hope of things getting better. Periodic adjustments of our expectations and attitudes helped us cope with the decline. The Internet and various books written about Alzheimer's can provide much information about what to expect. For instance, visit www.Alzheimer's.com.

A negative mind-set robs us of energy and creatively finding new coping skills. Every time we asked the question "How long must we endure?" the ultimate answer kept coming back: "Until God's purposes are fulfilled." We were reminded that even when endurance seems to have run its course, new insight may be just around the corner waiting to be tapped. The negative approach never generated a positive outcome.

We felt the need to guard "faith and hope," knowing that the prayers we uttered to the Lord would be useless if we kept carrying the load on our shoulders instead of leaving the burden with Him. While there is no imminent prospect of improvement with an Alzheimer's patient, there is always hope of finding better ways of coping with the disease. A lack of faith and hope leads to depression and possibly being out of control as a caregiver.

A lack of faith and hope also might lead to retreating from the battle, of giving up. It took a great deal of courage to face the enemy, but we were not alone. In fact, I Samuel 17:47 says "...for the battle is the Lord's...." Placing our confidence in Him removed doubt and gave us room to grow with the uncertainties of life, knowing His promises are always true. He is ever faithful and is the same yesterday, today, and forever (Hebrews 13:8). Were we the same? Could the Lord trust us with the circumstances we faced?

We also tend to limit what God wants to do through us if we are busy retreating from various problems rather than facing them. Paul tells us in Philippians 4:13 that "I can do all things through Christ who strengthens me." Victory is assured when we move by faith from "through me" to "through Christ." It is linking our limited selves to God's almightiness. To do less is like having a recipe and all the ingredients in place but mixing the batter with a spoon rather than plugging an electric mixer into electricity and using it.

We can function on our own, but no wonder life can be so discouraging. Power is available; we just need to plug in.

The Lord was not waiting for us to act in different or more desirable circumstances. He called us to be effective where we were, to learn what we could while there, and to cast our burdens upon Him. We were admonished to serve with joy rather than with fear or complaint. We were responsible for today, knowing that tomorrow might never come.

* * * * *

This section will address the givens that were in place at the beginning of our caregiving:

1. Excellent trust factor between Mom and us.
2. Had a good Christian background.
3. Good social skills with our church people and friends.
4. Excellent health, except for a lazy bowel, bunion, and corns.
5. Never complained about any food; maintained a healthy appetite.
6. Did not have false teeth.
7. Was not overweight.
8. Desires were pretty simple.
9. Did not question major or minor changes. She did not seem to be aware of them.
10. Maintained a good sense of humor.

11. Great appreciation for music.

12. Maintained a desire to be helpful even though the skills were no longer present. That was a plus and a minus as we tried to find things she could do.

* * * * *

The following discussion sets forth the practical coping skills we found helpful as related to the problems discussed in chapter five.

Loss of Organization

Because Mom sensed this problem at times, we felt she needed much reassurance that she was not alone and that all of her needs were being met. We tried to keep worry and anxiety at a minimum.

It was necessary that we be alert to the various losses that kept taking place so we could fill in the gaps and assist where needed. Downsizing was helpful in keeping things manageable for her as well as for us.

Confusion with Eating

Mom got to the point of needing assistance with her eating. Etiquette was not the issue as much as being sure she ate what was needed. She never complained about any food, however, and always maintained a healthy appetite, without putting on weight.

Since the knobs for our kitchen stove were not handy for Mom, we were not faced with the problem of potential fire in that area. It is something that must be addressed if appliances are convenient for an Alzheimer's individual.

Loss of Sense of Time

This requires a lot of repetition but should not be a big deal. Also, since it had become a habit for Mom to wear a watch, it was important to her that she always wear one. Whether it worked or not was not the issue; she just seemed to feel incomplete without it.

Dread of Being Alone

This became a plus for us because it reduced an otherwise independent spirit in Mom that might have been difficult to work with. She was quite content to rely on us for her needs.

Paranoia

We refrained from argument as reasoning did not go anywhere. We tried to reassure Mom that she was not alone. Many times we were able to change her environment, such as removing large mirrors from her room because of the "threatening people" reflected there for her. We also tried to avoid discussions with her that might lead to argument or paranoia.

Argumentation

We learned to join in with her imaginary world where helpful. Being right was not important in most of the conversations. Where safety became an issue, we restructured the difficult situation or would try to change the subject. Sometimes physical restraint became necessary, but usually a walk outside or a cup of hot chocolate would suffice.

Boredom

It became more and more difficult to entertain Mom as her attention span became less and less lengthy. In addition, her comprehension and understanding began to diminish causing television and reading to become boring. We faced new challenges every day as we tried to match her desires with her deteriorating skills. She wanted to be helpful and do something worthwhile.

Mom found satisfaction in doing simple housekeeping chores such as vacuuming or dusting. She also enjoyed working in the kitchen with setting the table, wiping dishes, or stirring ingredients on the stove. As long as everything was set out for her and simple directions were given, she could at least make an attempt at certain jobs. Folding clothes was another project that filled time. I had to keep in mind that the quality of work was not as important as giving her something to do. I could always go back and make corrections later.

Outside, Mom always enjoyed raking and picking up leaves. This required supervision as she no longer seemed to distinguish between flowers and weeds or leaves.

Almost daily we took two-mile walks around the area. She seemed to enjoy these immensely. Any repetition was viewed as new and refreshing.

For years Mom had a habit of doing crossword puzzles, so I bought books of them to always have on hand. When they became too difficult, we reduced down to word search puzzles. These held her interest until she was unable to recognize words and letters.

Wandering

We utilized several things to help us with the problem of wandering:

1. A permanent ID bracelet which included her name, our address and phone number, and the designation of Alzheimer's on it.
2. A security system in our home to let us know when windows or doors were violated.
3. Neighborhood awareness and cooperation.

Complaining/Negative Spirit

This spirit developed with the disease and increased in fervor. Our best response was to attend to what was needed and otherwise develop selective hearing or change the subject. Most outbursts or complaints were short-lived. Someone said "love is blind." A caregiver must be blind much of the time, overlooking the situation rather than reacting to it.

Loss of Appropriateness

Flexibility and reduced expectations go a long way in diffusing anger. In addition, embarrassment needs to be set aside because the Alzheimer's victim is doing the best he/she can. We did not find it difficult to take Mom out in public even though we could not always count on what behavior might surface. We found the general public was quite forgiving, and we were able to hold our head high. Never once did we find the onlooker having been offended. In fact, I believe they often showed admiration with the situation.

Disorientation

We found that familiarity brought the most comfort to Mom. Rearranging her bedroom, providing a new bedspread, new clothes, etc., unsettled her. Mom's stability was related to her recognition of things around her, and that was gradually disappearing.

Travel produced much disorientation because of the rapid changes going by; she could not process them. We learned early on not to take her on long trips.

Grocery shopping was enhanced when Mom took charge of pushing the cart around. It gave her a feeling of stability against the shelves of merchandise that she always thought were waiting to cave in on her.

Agitation and Hostility

This was short-lived with Mom, fortunately. Again, changing the subject or circumstances usually worked.

Catastrophize Pain

Mom's health tended to be excellent; she did not have a cold or flu in the four years she was with us. Alzheimer's generated confusion and a very low tolerance for pain. My test for sickness was that if the subject could be changed and the proposed pain disappeared, then I discounted it and went on with other things. If the pain persisted, which it never did, I would have dealt with the problem or sought professional help. Sometimes I would give her a Tylenol, hoping it would settle her down. At other times a placebo was helpful.

Catastrophize Noise

We learned to overlook her reactions to noise and tried to minimize problems. Mom needed reassurance as many normal sounds became foreign and sometimes hostile to her.

Obsessions

Bowels

Long-time habits are difficult to break with an Alzheimer's victim. Such was the case with Mom, who had a legitimate lazy bowel, but she was used to taking harsh laxatives or enemas. We restructured her treatment with Metamucil-type products, plenty of grains and cereals, prune juice, and plenty of liquids. I was forced to give her placebos in the form of Vitamin C to deal with her laxative obsession. It seemed to work well.

Carrying a purse

We realized early on that Mom needed to carry a purse because of another long-time habit but we removed anything of value so it would not create a dilemma if lost.

Wearing a wristwatch

Mom also needed to carry a wristwatch for the same reason as the purse.

Caring for her cat

It was necessary that we find a new home for the cat for its safety.

Mega desire to drive

Our case was simplified by the fact that Mom was driving with an illegal driver's license. She was long overdue for a Washington State driver's license since she had been a resident for two years already, but still carried a California driver's license. She never would have been able to pass a test so this problem took care of itself.

Aversion to hygiene

Assistance was required in this area, with a lot of just keepin' on and much overlooking of hostility.

Aversion to new things

Surrounding Mom with familiar things allowed us to slip in something different or new occasionally.

Pacing

I believe some of this stemmed from boredom or not knowing what to do. While I could not control it at night, sometimes taking her on a walk or trying to find something for her to do would suffice.

Loss of communication

Mom's speech began to fragment toward the end of her stay with us. We were able to communicate sufficiently, however, much as one would with a child. We tried to keep conversations in a soft tone and very simple.

Grinding teeth

This happened periodically day and night. Giving Mom gum to chew helped during the day. The nursing home continued this practice later on.

Chapter Seven

Transition To An Alzheimer's Care Center

⟨~~~⟩

One of my prayers was that we would be able to care for Mom at least until she no longer knew who we were or where she was. The Lord honored that prayer in the very best way possible and, as always, right on time. At this stage of non-recognition, the family bonding was no longer as significant to her. We knew that at some point in time we would be placing her in a care center, so we decided to put her name on a waiting list, which usually spanned about a year's time. It was quite a shock when an opening came within three months.

As a caregiver, it is easy to get so caught up with the needs of the patient that you lose sight of your own needs. Such was the case with me, and it did not really dawn on me until I was faced with the potential for relief. When the care center notified me of the opening, my first thought was that this was way too premature. I argued with the Lord, wanting to choose the time myself. And yet I knew if this time was not accepted, her name would go to the bottom of the list again. Would we need help before another year went by?

All of our circumstances were pointing in the direction of accepting the opening, but I was struggling to listen. My emotions kept interfering with reason. The thought of taking Mom somewhere to die played and on in my mind. Little did I know how hard the emotional separation would be after caring for her for four years. It was essential that this decision override the emotional side with a realization that time would heal the void.

Some of the facts that led us to finally say "yes" were: (1) the increased difficulty in caring for Mom; (2) the fact that better care was available for her than I could provide at that time; and (3) my physical health was deteriorating rapidly.

Arthritis was taking control of my right hip. At times the pain was so severe that when Neil wanted to help me, I could only respond, "Don't touch me." There did not seem to be any position or medication in which relief could be found. Prayer and trust in the Lord provided some degree of comfort. Other times, after preparing a meal, I sought peace in the hot tub and ate my dinner there. Common sense would say the Lord was very much on time with the new care option for Mom. He knew the whole picture so much better than I did, and all I needed to do was get my emotions out of the way.

In making our decision, it is helpful to note that we did a lot of research on nursing homes to find one that was not full of horror stories. The best way to find this out is by word of mouth, reputation, and actually going there with your own checklist. We were concerned with: the type and sufficiency of staff, the adequacy of the facility, whether there were bad odors, what the food was like, whether things were clean and sanitary, violations with the state, how the staff treated each other, and how the staff treated the most difficult patients. We were also interested in a secured Alzheimer's unit, providing both freedom and security for the patient.

The particular facility we chose had changed its name to specify "care center" rather than "nursing home." This suggested a more progressive and less negative attitude relative to this kind of institution. It had a good reputation and was large enough to have a special Alzheimer's unit for eighteen patients. It was a secured area that operated much like a big family unit. This was especially beneficial for Mom, having been the oldest of twelve children. She immediately thought the other patients were her siblings and began to treat them as such.

The special unit had a large activity/dining center; large double bedrooms; and a beautiful, large, secured outdoor courtyard. The only Alzheimer's patients in this unit were those who were ambulatory. When the patients became wheelchair bound and unable to roam, they were transferred to the main facility.

Having made the decision to move Mom to the care center, it was amazing how all of the details fell into place. Again the Lord was at work preparing every step. Certain types of clothes were recommended, and to my surprise, many of them were on a special sale that week. After packing the various things she would need, we placed her in the car and traveled to her new home. It was so very hard to say goodbye, but Mom didn't know this new place hadn't always been where she lived. There was no apparent adjustment for her to make. This was a great blessing to me because I did not want her to feel that we had abandoned her.

We were not to make contact with her for a couple of weeks so she could get fully oriented, but we called periodically to see how she was doing. It was "business as usual" for her, and we were never mentioned. What a relief to know she was content and not pining away.

On the other hand, I fought with tears for three weeks. Neil was so comforting, even suggesting we could bring her back home again. Somehow I was convinced the decision was the right one at the right time, but it took me a little while to work through a sort of grieving process. It helped a lot when we were able to visit her and see firsthand how she was getting along.

Mom always seemed glad to see us when we came, but seldom was there any recognition of who we were. I would bring photo albums of her childhood to review with her and any other things that might conjure up special memories. It was very hard to tell what she understood, but my conversations with her were as though she could comprehend everything. Sometimes she would try to make an appropriate response, so I never underestimated her ability to understand. I was aware of the fact, however, that she could not attend to very many words at a time. Simplicity was essential as her world kept getting smaller and smaller. It was always a joy to visit with her and see her contentment.

Then it was my turn. I went into the hospital for a total hip replacement. After the surgery, the doctor said there was nothing holding the bones together. The hip socket fell apart in his hands. How thankful I was then that Mom was being well cared for.

Chapter Eight

Involvement With The Care Center

Mom integrated well with all the others in the Alzheimer's unit and seemed to enjoy the interaction. It was amusing to hear some of the conversations between the patients. One day I was listening to a lady rattle on in nonsense syllables, and finally Mom looked up at her and asked, "Can you eat it?" The babble was not a problem for her and reminded me of small children learning to talk. What acceptance, as opposed to argument or criticism!

A small, extremely well-behaved dachshund was part of the unit. One day one of the aides mentioned to me that Mom all but drowned the dog trying to bathe it, head first, down in the sink. She thought she was in control and quite a tug of war ensued in trying to extricate the dog from the situation. Apparently the aides saw the humor of it all and enjoyed sharing the incident.

Another story was told about how Mom, who was playing the role of mother over all of the other patients, went to one of their beds in the night, pulled the person out of bed, yanked all the bedding onto the floor, and said, "Come on. We must get going." It was never determined where they were supposed to be going, but she was going to get there. The aide said things were back on track with little difficulty. Mom never tried to leave the facility and viewed it as her home. Even when we came for visits, she did not try to follow us out the door but went on with her imaginary business as usual.

I especially appreciated the family involvement that was encouraged by the care center. We were able to dine with Mom many times and enjoy activities along with her. The facility served excellent food which looked, as well as tasted, good. Tablecloths were used with linen napkins, nice dishes, and goblets. Sometimes I would bring several ladies with me for a surprise party. Mom would get so excited she would have trouble eating. Though she did not remember who people were, there seemed to be some kind of recognition. As time went by, however, I realized her inability to attend to more than one person or thing at a time.

Not long after Mom arrived at the care center, she became incontinent. Her speech continued to deteriorate to two or three words. Eventually she lost her ability to walk, talk, and feed herself. She was becoming a total care patient. At that point, she was transferred to the main section of the care center.

This shift was a sadness to us because we had grown so accustomed to the Alzheimer's unit. No longer would she experience the "family" ties and activities in the same way, but perhaps she was no longer able to benefit from them anyway.

We still came to visit often and to share with her whether she understood or not. While the conversations were one-sided, we still could get a chuckle out of her when discussing something funny. She maintained a wonderful sense of humor and could be made to laugh easily.

One day we were alerted to the fact that Mom had disappeared in the middle of the night, only to discover that she had fallen off the bed and rolled underneath. This was the beginning of the use of side rails.

In addition, after receiving about the tenth phone call of Mom falling out of her wheelchair, I requested she be secured in some way. Little did I know the state of Washington did not allow for restraints except by permission of the individual. Apparently belts were overused in the past to control patients, so it was outlawed. That does very little good for the person in need who is unable to speak for him or herself. Even my power of attorney for Mom was not accepted on this issue.

State regulations made little difference to me because the danger of falling was still there. Mom had a right to safety, not a right to fall. Surely a broken shoulder or hip should be avoided if possible, let alone the constant deep bruises. I was reminded of how we are required to use safety belts in an automobile but prohibited from using them in a care center.

The spills that kept occurring were not due to neglect on the part of the care center. They tried using wedged pillows that would force Mom back in the seat, but her tendency at that time was to lean forward as though trying to pick something off of the floor. Inevitably she would fall out.

It was interesting that the care center was in full agreement with me on the problem of a restraining belt, but they felt unable to comply. Rather than be intimidated by the state, I reemphasized the need and said I was willing to do whatever it would take to accomplish the goal, but "no" was not an option. I was ready to go to the governor, to the local TV stations, and to anyone else who could turn this around. My request had turned into a demand for compliance the next day.

It was interesting that a loophole was found, and Mom was with a safety belt within a few hours. A request was obtained from her doctor, and the care center felt comfortable with that. Rather than a reaction from her on the use of restraints, she actually seemed to be more relaxed. Perhaps she had a foreboding feeling of continually falling out of the wheelchair. It is unfortunate that common sense cannot be used because of past abuses. I wonder about the patients with special needs who have no one to speak up for them.

Overall, we were very pleased with the care Mom received. She was always clean and smelled good, no matter when we came for a visit. Physical therapy was given to her to help with the stiffening muscles. We noticed a respect and compassion given to any and all the patients when we were visiting.

Chapter Nine

Retirement And Relocation

About the time things were under control for Mom at the care center, it was time for us to retire. We had planned to move to the east side of the state, and it would involve moving her to a new facility as well.

We chose a convalescent center on the Colville Indian Reservation, which was only seven miles from where we would live. The surrounding area, which was dry and full of sage brush, was very similar to the terrain where she grew up. She would have had a great appreciation for the location if she could have comprehended it. So often in the past she shared loving and meaningful experiences of her childhood and where she lived.

The move would require a five and one-half hour trip. I was filled with apprehension as I thought of Mom's difficulty with travel. Neil would be driving another vehicle, so I would be transporting her alone. Could she sit that long in one place? What about her incontinence? Would I be able to stop for a break? What about lunch? Questions kept piling up, but again the Lord had all the answers in place before I even knew what to ask.

The paperwork was in place for the transition with very little difficulty. When I arrived to pick Mom up, she had already eaten breakfast, been cleaned up, and fitted with a temporary catheter. What a blessing! Answers were on the way, and I didn't even know such things were available. In addition, knowing her disorientation, the care center provided me with a container of applesauce and a sedative to be used if necessary.

The Lord had a much better plan in mind, and the sedative was never used. A cassette of George Beverly Shea's most recent gospel songs was given to us as a going-away present. Knowing how much Mom always loved music, this seemed an ideal way to keep her attention and help her relax. He was a favorite singer of mine as well.

When we got onto the freeway, the first song in the group was, "I'd Rather Have Jesus." Mom immediately showed signs of joyful recognition as she moved back and forth in the seat for a few minutes saying, "Oh, oh, oh." This cassette was the key to the success of the trip. It is a wonder it was not completely worn out by the time we got there.

After a few miles on the road, Mom began to fidget with the catheter which brought me great concern. Remembering a pile of clothes in the back seat, I quickly grabbed some and put them on her lap. This seemed to suffice. It gave her something to do in addition to listening to music.

Rather than worry about a lunch, I had crackers along and stopped to give Mom a drink from time to time. She never fell asleep on the trip but seemed to enjoy the travel, which surprised me. I was constantly reminded of the Lord's presence and care for both of us. Again He was synchronizing "all things together" for good and meeting our needs at every turn.

Chapter Ten

Home On The Colville Indian

⧽⧽⧽⧽⧽

RESERVATION

Mom's deterioration continued, and with it came new problems. Even though I had not been the primary caregiver for some time, many decisions required my attention, such as with the restraint belt. It was necessary that I keep alert and not take the care for granted.

Both institutions requested that I fill out forms directing them on whether they should use artificial means to prolong the life of Mom, should it have become necessary. This is a very difficult issue to process.

A person may not believe in euthanasia or infanticide, but the question might be asked, "Is there a point in which we might be interfering with God's natural process of death by keeping an individual alive only by artificial means?" The decision could be made for us and be out of our hands, however, if the patient has signed a "living will" requesting no artificial supports be used to sustain life.

Fortunately most nursing home forms are not locked in concrete but can be changed at will. This gives a person time to reassess the situation. Such was the case with Mom. She was losing her mental ability to swallow food or liquid. She was going on her tenth year with Alzheimer's, had been wheelchair bound for several years, and was unable to carry on a conversation except with an occasional utterance. She continued to show some degree of recognition with some communication and music, however. She was seldom sick or fraught with pain. Since God is the author of invention and true science, would I be assuming His role by allowing her to starve to death rather than providing her with artificial feeding through a shunt?

Mom did not have a "living will," and I doubt that she would have wanted artificial supports. On the other hand, I don't believe she would have fancied starvation. Our decision was to elongate her life, realizing that with God's timing, not even artificial supports would hold death at bay.

We continue to make her life as meaningful as possible, realizing again that God's purposes are bigger than Mom or us. Praise the Lord for His direction and the peace that always accompanies it.

Another reason for choosing "life" for Mom was the wonderful care she received at the convalescent center. She endeared herself to the staff, making it a joy to care for her. One day I remember scheduling a short haircut for her, and various aides intervened saying, "Please let her hair grow longer. She would look wonderful in French braids." I didn't even know how to make a French braid. How special that they would take that kind of time.

One sunny afternoon, I stopped by to take Mom for a stroll. Already someone was carting her around, and she was wearing a lovely big sun bonnet. These people always spend quality time with the patients. Residents who were able were bussed on fishing trips, to fairs, and on many other excursions. Holidays were always celebrated with a big splash with family members encouraged to attend. There would be decorations, music, and entertainment, as well as lots of good food.

Each Christmas celebration was overwhelming as we observed the extremely generous spirit of the Native Americans. Patients' names were drawn by the staff and other Native Americans living in the area. It seemed that every resident received at least half a dozen very meaningful gifts. Of Mom's gifts this year, two were very elaborate music boxes, one playing "Jesus Loves Me" and the other playing "Beautiful Dreamer." What ideal gifts! I play them often when sitting by her bed.

In addition, whenever powwows were held at the facility, we noticed the extreme amount of respect that was paid to the elderly from the youngest children to the adults. The

Native Americans have a special regard for "elders," regardless of their nationality. Small children were taught to greet the patients with a handshake and a smile.

Further deterioration of Mom's muscles took place at this institution. It made dressing her more and more difficult, so I began buying larger sweat suits. In addition, I slit the tops down the back, seamed the edges and added velcro closings. Dresses also worked well this way. Instead of a coat for winter, a cape can be made to fit around the individual rather than trying to work with the stiff arms. Since Mom has not walked for some time, we use slippers in the winter and slip-on tennis shoes in the summer.

We have always appreciated the cleanliness of the convalescent center because of all of the incontinent patients. Few, if any, are on catheters, yet seldom is anyone wet. This can only be attributed to a highly motivated staff of caring aides and professionals.

Chapter Eleven

Ministry In Disguise

CRIIIO

Paul mentions in II Corinthians 3:2-3 that "You are our epistle written in our hearts, known and read by all men; you are manifestly an epistle of Christ, ministered by us, written not with ink but by the Spirit of the living God, not on tablets of stone but on tablets of flesh, that is, of the heart."

What an awesome thought, that whether we like it or not, whether we are effective or not, our lives are like a book being read by those around us. I wonder what other people read about my life. Does what they see compel them to look beyond me to Christ?

It is obvious that the Lord plants people where He wants them to minister and not particularly with regard to the person's choosing. It took a whale to get Jonah's attention and bodily transport him to Ninevah.

Joseph, while yet a lad, was sold to Midianite traders by his brothers. God intervened, and Joseph ended up as ruler over Pharaoh's house and all his people. Only in regard to the throne was Pharaoh greater than Joseph (see Genesis 41:37-40). After a famine occurred in the land, Joseph's brothers went to Egypt for grain, not knowing they would be at their brother's mercy. The end of the story shows great compassion when Joseph responds: "But now, do not therefore be grieved or angry with yourselves because you sold me here; for God sent me before you to preserve life" (Genesis 45:5). "And God sent me before you to preserve a posterity for you in the earth, and to save your lives by a great deliverance. So now it was not you who sent me here, but God" (Genesis 45:7-8a).

While I have not always purposed ministry in every circumstance, when I sought Him and His direction, ministry happened in spite of myself because it was His Holy Spirit that worked in and through me. Nursing homes would never have been a point of outreach without my being forced into the circumstances. This book would never have been written without Alzheimer's invading my life.

David said it so well in Psalm 37:23 that "The steps of a good man are ordered by the Lord, and He delights in his way." This verse energized me to maximize the situations around me and challenged me to become an opportunist for the Lord, rather than waiting for something more exciting or palatable to happen before I began to function.

My intellect could never put the galaxies together nor could it hold them in space. Neither do I tell the birds where to build their nests or remind the flowers to bloom again in the spring. Who am I to presume upon God's wisdom? Who am I to bring counsel or argument to Him?

How easy it is to want to choose and control the experiences in which we bring praise to Him, rather than accepting the challenge that is before us and trusting Him with the details. Perhaps, in His wisdom and timing, we have all of the information we can handle for the moment. In His love, He may be protecting us from overload by not requiring all of the lessons to be learned at once. He knows our limitations and our humanity better than we do, as well as our potential. I needed to trust Him with that information.

The Bible tells us that our purpose for being on this earth is to bring praise to him. David responds in Psalm 34:1 "I will bless the Lord at all times; His praise shall continually be in my mouth." The writer in Hebrews 13:15 admonishes us with "Therefore by Him let us continually offer the sacrifice of praise to God, that is, the fruit of our lips, giving thanks to His name."

These verses are well and good. It is easy to praise God when things are going positively, but what happens when the going gets rough? When bad things happen to good people? Our journey with Alzheimer's was either just one to be endured or one to be filled with victory, peace, and joy. Praise the Lord, it was the latter in spite of the gross deterioration.

Philippians 4:7 was of great comfort to me. "The peace of God which surpasses all understanding, will guard your hearts and minds through Christ Jesus." I was persuaded, with Paul in Romans 8:38-39 "...that neither death nor life, nor angels nor principalities nor powers, nor things present nor things to come, nor height nor depth, nor any other created thing, shall be able to separate us from the love of God which is in Christ Jesus our Lord." How exciting to realize those verses included Mom.

Some people wonder why a loving God would allow a disease such as Alzheimer's, especially where praise is no longer able to come from the lips of a senile Christian. John 9:2-3 gives some insight in a dialogue between Jesus and His disciples over "...who sinned, this man or his parents, that he was born blind?" Jesus answered, "Neither this man nor his parents sinned, but that the works of God should be revealed in him."

Time and again we hear stories of how the Lord blessed and brought great joy out of tremendous affliction. People have been literally "used up" for His glory. While the mind may no longer be intact, an individual's presence may speak volumes for the Lord, and we who look on may be the vehicle through which He wants to work. God knows the heart even when the mind is disengaged.

Our faith was made to bloom as we trusted God moment by moment and experienced His love, grace, and mercy. The key was keeping our focus on Christ. I was often reminded of Peter who began to "sink" when he took his eyes off of Christ and placed them back on the impossible situation before him. I was also reminded of Paul who was able to let go of the troubling "thorn in his side" when he heard Jesus say (and took Him at His word), "My grace is sufficient for you, for My strength is made perfect in weakness" (II Corinthians 12:9a).

It was this philosophy that turned our home into a mission station and both of the nursing homes into a mission field. We are seldom aware of the "fruit of our labors," but the results are always the Lord's anyway. Seeds were planted through home Bible studies, music programs, faithfulness, compassion, joy in spite of circumstances, and example. You can always look back and think of many ways you could have done things better, but Psalm 37:23 kept running through my mind about our steps being ordered of the Lord. If that is the case, there is no better place to be and our part is simply being faithful. Satan would have us dwell on our limitations and inadequacies, but "I can do all things through Christ who strengthens me" (Philippians 4:13) – that is, all things that He has equipped me for and that need to be done.

The first care center for Mom was located twenty miles from where we lived in Auburn, which made it difficult to get very involved. We did, however, have weekly visits and tried to relate with the staff and other patients where possible.

Sometimes I would stop and pray with an individual even though he/she might not have understood. The main thing was that the Lord always understood and cared for each one.

The convalescent center on the Colville Indian Reservation was a different story. First of all, it was close at hand and the facility was much smaller, allowing for a more intimate atmosphere. Sixty beds were available and everyone was integrated, much like a large family. There were no separate units, so everyone was able to participate in activities.

Soon after placing Mom at the center, I began to volunteer for a music program once a week. Many times it featured hymn arrangements and other times a mixture of old familiar tunes and meaningful verse. At times I would involve the patients in sing-alongs, games of "name that tune," and ask key questions of the period in which the song was written, such as "Who was president?"

It was not long before a neighbor of ours was placing her mother-in-law in the same care center. She, too, was a Christian and decided to join me in the music. This was extra special to me because I was not a soloist but more into harmony and the keyboard. How I longed for the words to be shared, especially the hymns. These people were closer to eternity than anyone else and needed to hear the Gospel. As a team we could be so much more effective.

Many were the times we would go into rooms and pray with patients or try to bring some joy into their lives. Some were so appreciative that they would give us homemade gifts. This always made me uncomfortable as I thought of how little they had to give. I began to realize, however, how much it meant for them to know someone cared enough to spend time with them. Quite often I would have migraine headaches and be tempted to stay home, but again, any pain or struggles I had were nothing compared to their need for someone to be there.

God is so good! A new couple moved in across the road from us and began attending our Bible studies. The wife became very interested in helping with our music program at the convalescent center and began to take charge every other month. This gave us some time off and kept the bases covered.

It was exciting when various patients would try to sing along with the music, try to remember song titles, and respond to historical questions. Sometimes they were a bit hysterical instead and would generate a lot of laughter.

Of special interest were the responses that came from some of the staff. They, too, got involved with the singing and recall. One time I was playing an arrangement of "Turn Your Eyes Upon Jesus." A most unlikely aide began to sing the words as he left the room. It was a great surprise to me that he knew the song.

I hope this book will bring praise to our wonderful, loving Lord in spite of our tragedy. "I will bless the Lord at all times;

His praise shall continually be in my mouth, my soul shall make its boast in the Lord;...But those who seek the Lord shall not lack any good thing" (Psalm 34:1-2, 10b). "I will sing of the mercies of the Lord forever; with my mouth will I make known Your faithfulness to all generations" (Psalm 89:1).

What does it mean to minister in disguise? Perhaps it can be summed up by saying that no matter what form it takes, His Word will not return void (see Isaiah 55:11). He will accomplish that which He purposes especially when His ministry becomes our ministry. How privileged we are to be a part of it! PRAISE THE LORD!

Chapter Twelve

Scientific Data

What is Alzheimer's Disease?

"Alzheimer's disease is a brain disorder which gradually destroys the ability to reason, remember, imagine, and learn. It's different from the mild forgetfulness normally observed in older people. Over the course of the disease, people with Alzheimer's no longer recognize themselves or much about the world around them. Depression, anxiety, and paranoia often accompany these symptoms. Although there is no cure, new treatments help lessen Alzheimer's symptoms and slow its progression" (www.Alzheimer's.com). Visit the site for more information.

The Progression of Alzheimer's

These steps are based on Mom's actual decline:

1. Loss of organization
2. Confusion with eating

3. Loss of sense of time

4. Dread of being alone

5. Paranoia

6. Argumentation

7. Boredom

8. Wandering

9. Complaining/negative spirit

10. Loss of appropriateness

11. Disorientation

12. Agitation and hostility

13. Catastrophize pain

14. Catastrophize noise

15. Obsessions

16. Aversion to hygiene

17. Aversion to new things

18. Pacing

19. Loss of communication

20. Grinding teeth

21. Loss of recognition

22. Loss of ability to walk

23. Inability to swallow food and drink

This page shows a comparative scale, called the "Functional Assessment Staging (FAST) scale," which was developed by Barry Reisberg, M.D., and colleagues in 1984. It charts the decline of people with Alzheimer's disease (from www.Alzheimer's.com).

Functional Assessment Staging (FAST) Scale

FAST Scale Stage	Characteristics
1. Normal adult.	No functional decline.
2. Normal older adult.	Personal awareness of some functional decline.
3. Early Alzheimer's disease.	Noticeable deficits in demanding job situations.
4. Mild Alzheimer's.	Requires assistance in complicated tasks such as handling finances and planning parties.
5. Moderate Alzheimer's.	Requires assistance in choosing proper attire.
6. Moderately severe Alzheimer's.	Requires assistance in dressing, bathing, and toileting. Has urinary and fecal incontinence.
7. Severe Alzheimer's.	Speech ability declines to about a half dozen intelligible words. Progressive loss of abilities to walk, sit up, smile, and hold head up.

Treatment for Alzheimer's

There is no known cure, but there is a great deal of optimism as research comes closer and closer to effective treatments. Log onto www.Alzheimer's.com for some of the conventional and alternative treatments that are being used at this time. Check the Internet periodically for new updated material. Hope is around the corner.

People may have Alzheimer's up to twenty years but usually die from some other disease such as pneumonia or the flu. Regardless, those with Alzheimer's tend to diminish on a steady basis until they are reduced to the "infancy stage." Even so, the Lord is still mindful of his own!

References

All Scripture quotations were taken from the New King James Version of the Bible.

Reisberg, Barry M.D., et al. (Functional Assessment Staging FAST scale), 1984.

Reprinted with permission from www.Alzheimer's.com, a member of the PlanetRx.com family of health-related websites.

Epilog

Much has been learned about the causation, potential treatment, and possible prevention of Alzheimer's Disease over the last few decades. Unfortunately, causes are still vague but promising research is now revealing new clues that are uncovering possible break-throughs in our understanding of the disease.

A rich treasure trove of information can be readily found by going on the internet and signing in to www.WebMd.com and writing in the Search Box: "Alzheimer's Disease". There, you will find links to hundreds of reputable professional articles that lay out clear facts that will help you understand the complexities of the disease.

With the Lord's help it is our prayer that you may find encouragement and effective counsel and effective help for your loved one!

Sincerely,
M. Joanne Roth

Printed and bound by PG in the USA

USA20199G0IL